46294547R00057

Made in the USA
Lexington, KY
24 July 2019